CONCOCTIONS

50 spellbinding cocktails

Millie Mercier

CONCOCTIONS

50 spellbinding cocktails

Illustrated by Kelly Smith

Smith Street Books

CONTENTS

Introduction 6

Cocktails as spellwork 8

Love 10

Strength 32

Vision 54

Luck 76

Harmony 98

Infusions & syrups 120

Index 134

Magic is all around you. It's in the earth, the sky, and the leaves clinging to their branches. It's in the bloom of a sunflower, turning to trace the path of the sun. It's in the roots of an apple tree, twining deep into the earth. It's in the fresh scent of mint and in the sweet taste of a ripe plum. It's in the moon's phases and the change of seasons.

Magic is in you.

This book is for those who recognise that magic is everywhere, accessible through a personal connection with the natural world and the bounty it provides. The kitchen witch practises her magic through everyday rituals that work with that abundance, whether through the miracle of a rising bread loaf or the potent charm of a perfectly mixed drink.

For the witch, intention is everything. Performing actions with deep and conscious awareness invites extraordinary effects. This type of magical practice requires nothing more than household goods and common ingredients, like the ones that fill this book, from cherries, with their romantic association, to ginger with its fiery ability to stoke power.

Each ingredient in your kitchen and garden has unique correspondences to the energies of the universe. The kitchen witch understands this and picks the elements of spells and offerings based on their magical properties.

This book's drinks are designed to harness these energies, created with ingredients that correspond to specific intentions: Love, Strength, Vision, Luck and Harmony. In the back of the book, you'll find recipes for infusions and syrups, which you can craft at home to deepen the resonance between your spells and the energies you'd like to invoke.

As you work through these recipes, treat them like a ritual. Each step of the preparation is an opportunity to imbue your ingredients with intention. Everything you do – from brewing a syrup to adding a final floral garnish – is part of your spell.

DRINK DEEPLY. THE MAGIC IS ALL AROUND YOU.

INTRODUCTION

COCKTAILS AS SPELLWORK

The practice of kitchen witchcraft allows you to harness the energies of the world seen and unseen to manifest your desires, whether you'd like to bring harmony to your home or invoke the help of a chosen deity. Each recipe in this book is designed to help you tap into these powers and deepen your connection to the universe and all of its mysteries.

As you prepare, mix and create cocktails, you can infuse each ingredient with your will. Through this practice and the conscious combination of herbs, fruit, flowers and extracts, specially chosen for their magical correspondences, the cocktails you brew become the embodiment of your intention, to offer to your chosen deities or to consume.

To prepare your kitchen and yourself for spellwork, here are a few things to consider:

PREPARING YOUR SPACE & TOOLS
Help your magic achieve its full effect by cleansing your workspace before you begin.

Take the time to clear the space and its energies. You may wish to use bells and chimes, burn candles, sprinkle cleansing oils or place crystals around the room, depending on your preference and what tools you have available.

However, it isn't just your surrounds that matter: the most important factor is a calm inner environment. No matter what's going on around you, it's your mindset that will help to realise your spell and to work your will.

CHOOSING YOUR TIMING
You can enhance your craft by engaging with nature's rhythms, preparing your spells in time with the moon's phases or the passing of seasons and solstices.

For example, you can enhance the potency of a spell intended to bring about harmony by brewing it on an equinox, when day and night are of equal length, and the earth's energies are in perfect balance. Or you might prepare a spell to guide you through a big change when the moon is new – a time best suited for beginnings.

The energy of every ingredient you work with is connected to the universe's ebbs and flows, from the movement of the planets to the ticking of the clock. Magic is a part of nature and flows with, not against it.

FOCUSING YOUR ENERGY
As you brew your syrups, prepare your garnishes and mix your drinks, focus on your magical intention. You may wish to hold a mantra or words of power in your head to reinforce your focus, which you can recite as you hold each ingredient, slice through each peel and muddle each herb.

As you work, visualise your goal. Consider it already so. The more you focus your energy and intention while you prepare your drinks, the greater the magical effects of your spells will be.

STORE BOUGHT OR HOMEMADE?
You will find that some recipes in this book call for ingredients like rose petal syrup or cherry-infused gin.

While these syrups and infusions may be available to buy from the store, making them from scratch can deepen your connection to each element of a spell, as you are able to imbue the ingredients more fully with your will.

These recipes are located at the back of this book. If you do choose to create your own infusions and syrups, ensure you store your creations in containers that have been washed with hot, soapy water and dried before use.

LOVE

To ignite a spark.
To deepen a connection.
To open the heart to new possibilities.
To foster self-love.
To connect to your deepest desires.
To embrace sensuality.
To channel a universal flowering.
To amplify love in all its forms.

Love is a universal life force, binding us together. When you connect to yourself in a profound way, you may find that a blossoming occurs.

Love is everywhere. Drink deeply and usher it in.

SOLSTICE SPARKLER

Invite romance into your life with this cherry-spiked potion – the perfect mix of sweetness and effervescence. The fruit's deep ties to the heart, paired with a cleansing, happiness-inducing squeeze of lemon, attracts love in all its forms. Garnish with the reddest cherry you can find.

ice cubes

30 ml (1 oz) Cherry gin (page 124)

15 ml (½ oz) Simple syrup (page 128)

15 ml (½ oz) lemon juice

chilled sparkling rosé, to top

cherry on a cocktail stick, to garnish

Fill a cocktail shaker with ice and add the cherry gin, simple syrup and lemon juice. Shake vigorously for 30 seconds, then strain into a chilled coupe glass.

Top up with the rosé and garnish with the cherry on the cocktail stick.

TRANSFIXER

With a beautiful golden hue, this drink captures the intoxicating spirit of being putting under the spell of another. Apricot is energetically tied to both love and peace, while pineapple offers protection. Paired together, they open the heart without placing it in danger. Best drunk on a Friday, the day sacred to Venus.

ice cubes

45 ml (1½ oz) white or light gold rum

10 ml (¼ oz) apricot liqueur

30 ml (1 oz) pineapple juice

15 ml (½ oz) lime juice

15 ml (½ oz) agave syrup

pineapple wedge, to garnish

Fill a cocktail shaker with ice and add the rum, apricot liqueur, pineapple juice, lime juice and agave syrup. Shake well for 30 seconds.

Strain into a chilled coupe glass and garnish with the pineapple wedge.

DUALITY

Smoky mezcal, bittersweet Campari and vegetal Zucca combine in this complex recipe that summons both earth's and fire's energies. Chinese rhubarb's presence in Zucca works with Campari's oranges, mezcal's agave and the chocolate bitters to invoke romance that scintillates and inspires the drinker to reconnect to their own power.

ice cubes, plus 1 large ice cube

30 ml (1 oz) mezcal

30 ml (1 oz) Zucca

30 ml (1 oz) Campari

3 dashes mole bitters

orange slice, to garnish

Fill a mixing glass with ice and add the mezcal, Zucca, Campari and mole bitters. Stir briskly.

Place the large ice cube in a tumbler and strain in the drink. Garnish with the orange slice.

FIRE SPARKER

The stimulating power of ginger comes together with sharp lime and sweet agave for a cocktail that stokes the passions. Ginger serves to boost the power of your magical intentions, its energies just the thing to imbibe in when you need a jolt of vital fire to manifest your will.

4 small chunks fresh pineapple

60 ml (2 oz) Ginger tequila (page 126)

15 ml (½ oz) lime juice

10 ml (¼ oz) agave syrup

ice cubes

chilled ginger beer, to top

crystallised ginger on a cocktail stick, to garnish

Place the pineapple chunks in a tall, chilled glass with the ginger tequila, lime juice and agave syrup and gently crush with a muddling tool. Stir to combine.

Add ice, top up with ginger beer and garnish with the crystallised ginger on the cocktail stick.

LOVE

CHALICE OF EROS

Strawberries have long been associated with love, perhaps because of their resemblance to the human heart. Here, the sweet fruit is muddled with fragrant basil and purifying lemon for an effervescent drink that encourages harmony and strength in relationships.

3 strawberries

2 basil leaves

15 ml (½ oz) lemon juice

60 ml (2 oz) vodka

ice cubes

chilled sparkling water, to top

Hull two of the strawberries and cut them into quarters. Place in a cocktail shaker with the basil leaves and lemon juice and gently crush with a muddling tool. Add the vodka and ice and shake well for 15 seconds.

Strain into a tall, chilled glass filled with ice and top up with sparkling water. Garnish with the remaining strawberry.

BLOOMING ELIXIR

Violet entwines with the transformative power of butterfly pea flowers for a drink that takes on an exquisite purple hue, as rare as a blue moon. The blooms combine to offer a healing, renewing presence, perfect for the growth of self-love, with a steadying influence that amplifies insights of the heart.

ice cubes

20 ml (¾ oz) Butterfly pea gin (page 122)

20 ml (¾ oz) creme de violette

20 ml (¾ oz) triple sec

20 ml (¾ oz) lemon juice

edible violet, to garnish

Fill a cocktail shaker with ice and pour in the butterfly pea gin, creme de violette, triple sec and lemon juice. Shake well for 30 seconds.

Strain into a chilled coupe glass and garnish with the violet.

PHILTRE OF VENUS

This spell inspires a sweetening of the heart and invites beauty and abundance in. The stone fruit kernels distilled into creme de noyaux infuse cream's fertile energy, working with chocolate's and cognac's romantic qualities for a potent combination best drunk as the moon begins to wax to harness its powers of growth.

ice cubes

20 ml (¾ oz) creme de noyaux

20 ml (¾ oz) white creme de cacao

15 ml (½ oz) cognac

45 ml (1½ oz) double (heavy) cream

2 maraschino cherries, to garnish

Fill a cocktail shaker with ice and pour in the creme de noyaux, creme de cacao, cognac and cream. Shake vigorously for 30 seconds.

Strain into a chilled coupe glass and garnish with the maraschino cherries.

NEW BEGINNINGS

This elegant cocktail marries gentian and juniper with happiness-inducing nasturtiums for a tipple that invites a flowering of love – drink when you wish to embark on a new phase in your romantic life. The botanicals of the alcohols encourage both love and strength to flourish as the past is cleansed and the future is entered with courage.

4 edible nasturtium flowers

ice cubes, plus 1 large ice cube

40 ml (1¼ oz) dry gin

30 ml (1 oz) Lillet Blanc

30 ml (1 oz) Suze (or similar gentian-based liqueur)

Place three of the nasturtiums in a mixing glass and gently crush with a muddling tool. Add ice and the gin, Lillet Blanc and Suze and stir briskly.

Place the large ice cube in a tumbler and strain in the drink. Garnish with the remaining nasturtium flower.

UNIVERSAL FLOWERING

Roses are a powerful symbol of the feminine divine. In this reinvention of the martini, the bloom elevates the drink with its beautifying energy. The rose is equally suited to the myriad forms of love, as it comes in many colours – for new romance, make the syrup with red petals, for self-love, call on pink, and for deepening friendships, use yellow.

ice cubes

50 ml (1¾ oz) gin

20 ml (¾ oz) dry vermouth

10 ml (¼ oz) Rose syrup (page 129)

2–3 drops orange bitters

edible rose petal, to garnish

Fill a cocktail shaker with ice and add the gin, vermouth and rose syrup. Shake well for 30 seconds, then strain into a chilled martini glass.

Garnish with the orange bitters and a rose petal.

MIDWINTER MULLED WINE

In this warming midwinter brew, star anise brings luck and enhances power, while cinnamon provides courage and the cloves increase attraction. These elements come together with the love-inducing qualities of orange and sugar to make enough wine to serve a coven. A batch may be used to help strengthen community and forge deeper bonds.

3 oranges

6 cloves, plus an extra 20 cloves to garnish

1.5 litres (51 oz) red wine

60 ml (2 oz) brandy

115 g (½ cup) brown sugar

3 cinnamon sticks

4 star anise

Cut one of the oranges into 10 wedges. Pierce each wedge with two cloves and set aside.

Juice the two remaining oranges and pour the juice into a saucepan. Add the rest of the ingredients and, taking care as alcohol is flammable, gently warm over medium heat until steaming, then reduce the heat to low and steep for a further 5 minutes. The wine will become more spiced the longer you warm it, so remove from the heat once it's reached your desired flavour.

Serve in heatproof mugs or glasses, garnishing each with a clove-studded orange slice.

STRENGTH

To connect to inner fortitude.
To face your fears. To act with conviction.
To maintain clarity. To honour a good habit.
To heighten resolve.
To cultivate energy. To boost confidence.
To accomplish whatever you
put your mind to.

Strength is not just about the
physical body. It's also about the mind,
the heart and the soul.

Find strength by connecting to the
deep energies of the earth and
the bounty it provides.

You already have everything you need.

DRAUGHT OF COURAGE

Step into the unknown with the fortifying effects of black tea, used to promote courage. The other ingredients in this spell can help create harmony and release, their presence a boon to lighten your load as you step into a new phase of life. For an extra boost of confidence, drink on Tuesday to tap into the energy of Mars.

5 g (¼ oz) black tea leaves

200 ml (7 oz) near-boiling water

30 ml (1 oz) calvados

15 ml (½ oz) Honey syrup (page 128)

10 ml (¼ oz) lemon juice

1 cinnamon stick

Steep the tea leaves in the hot water for 3–5 minutes, depending on how strong you like your tea. Strain into a teacup or heatproof glass, pour in the calvados, honey syrup and lemon juice and stir to combine.

Garnish with the cinnamon stick.

INNER WARD

Protective, fiery energies imbue this play on a Manhattan. Bourbon is primarily made from corn, nocino from walnut, these liquors bolstering each other to create an inner shield for drinkers. Layered on top are ingredients that can help to heighten happiness and connection to self for a draught that encourages and protects our inner voice.

ice cubes, plus 1 large ice cube

45 ml (1½ oz) bourbon

10 ml (¼ oz) vermouth rosso

10 ml (¼ oz) nocino

10 ml (¼ oz) sherry

dash of chocolate bitters

dash of orange bitters

walnut, to garnish

Fill a cocktail shaker with ice and add the bourbon, vermouth, nocino, sherry, chocolate bitters and orange bitters. Shake well for 30 seconds.

Place the large ice cube in a tumbler and strain in the drink. Garnish with the walnut.

SABBATH SANGAREE

Known as the king of the forest, the venerable oak tree imparts its strength in this historical cocktail. When preparing it, ensure you use brandy and port aged in oak barrels to capture the tree's magic. Layered on top is nutmeg, which deepens the drink's layers. Prepare on Midsummer for a more potent effect.

ice cubes

60 ml (2 oz) brandy

30 ml (1 oz) port

10 ml (¼ oz) Simple syrup (page 128)

grated nutmeg, to garnish

blood orange slice, to garnish

Fill a cocktail shaker with ice and add the brandy, port and simple syrup. Shake for 30 seconds, then strain into a chilled cocktail glass.

Garnish with a dusting of nutmeg and the blood orange slice.

SPICED BREW

Tap into your inner fire with this bold and invigorating brew that stokes black tea's strength-giving properties. Cinnamon and ginger mingle with the other chai spices, including black pepper, to cultivate powerful and vital energy. Drink when you'd like fortification to pursue your passions, whether that's working on an old project or a new creative endeavour.

ice cubes

60 ml (2 oz) vodka

45 ml (1½ oz) Chai syrup (page 133)

1 teaspoon finely grated ginger

chilled ginger beer, to top

cinnamon stick, to garnish

star anise, to garnish

Fill a cocktail shaker with ice and add the vodka, chai syrup and ginger. Shake well for 30 seconds, then strain into a mule mug filled with ice.

Top up with ginger beer and garnish with the cinnamon stick and star anise.

STRENGTH

BLOOD AND FIRE

The blood orange's red hue summons both strength and courage. Saffron deepens these fiery energies, twining with them to create a vitalising union that promotes confidence. Salt offers its protection and enhances this concoction's sweet and sour notes, for a creation that can help you access your inner fire.

1 teaspoon salt

1 blood orange or lime wedge

ice cubes

45 ml (1½ oz) tequila

15 ml (½ oz) triple sec

30 ml (1 oz) blood orange juice

10 ml (¼ oz) lime juice

10 ml (¼ oz) Saffron syrup (page 133)

saffron threads, to garnish

Place the salt on a small plate. Run the citrus wedge around the rim of a chilled tumbler, then dip the rim of the tumbler in the salt to coat.

Fill a cocktail shaker with ice and add the tequila, triple sec, blood orange juice, lime juice and saffron syrup. Shake well for 30 seconds.

Add ice to the tumbler and strain in the drink. Garnish with saffron threads.

SOLAR RAY

This citrus-infused cocktail invites protection. If negativity is pressing, the juniper from the gin, the orange from the Campari, and the tangerine can all encourage positive solar vibrations. This vibrant elixir is the perfect drink when you need to boost your intentions and encourage self-confidence; mix on a Sunday to channel extra solar energy.

20 ml (¾ oz) Campari

20 ml (¾ oz) sweet vermouth

20 ml (¾ oz) gin

30 ml (1 oz) tangerine juice

ice cubes, plus 1 large ice cube

tangerine wedge, to garnish

Fill a cocktail shaker with ice and pour in the Campari, vermouth, gin and tangerine juice. Shake well for 30 seconds.

Place the large ice cube in a tumbler and strain in the drink. Garnish with the tangerine wedge.

ALIGNMENT

Ginger is regarded for its ability to boost magical energy, lending spells heat. Drawing from Mars's determination, the root works with the fire of tequila to fill one's cup with power. A salt rim balances out the sweetness of the agave and offers a protective finish to help ground you in your goal.

1 teaspoon salt

2 lime wedges

ice cubes

60 ml (2 oz) Ginger tequila (page 126)

30 ml (1 oz) lime juice

15 ml (½ oz) agave syrup

Place the salt on a small plate. Run one lime wedge around the rim of a chilled tumbler, then dip the rim of the tumbler in the salt to coat.

Fill a cocktail shaker with ice and add the ginger tequila, lime juice and agave syrup. Shake well for 30 seconds.

Add ice to the tumbler and strain in the drink. Garnish with the second lime wedge.

BOUNTY'S BRAMBLE

Creme de mure is made with blackberries, a fruit fit to prepare for the festival of Lammas, as the year passes into summer's second half. The protection the berry offers is bolstered in this bramble by mulberry and rosemary. Together, they celebrate abundance and offer strength for seasons when harvests don't go to plan.

7 mulberries

50 ml (1¾ oz) Mulberry gin (page 122)

20 ml (¾ oz) lemon juice

20 ml (¾ oz) Rosemary syrup (page 130)

crushed ice

20 ml (¾ oz) creme de mure

Place four of the mulberries in a cocktail shaker. Pour in the mulberry gin, lemon juice and rosemary syrup, then use a muddling tool to firmly crush the berries. Shake well for 15 seconds, then strain into a chilled tumbler filled with crushed ice.

Drizzle the creme de mure over the ice, so that it trickles down. Garnish with the remaining three mulberries.

WITCHES' BOULEVARDIER

With its sharp points, the artichoke is a thistle that embodies protection and is useful for courage. It is used to produce Cynar, which introduces Mars's energy to this play on the boulevardier. The grains in the whisky and grapes in the vermouth mix in Earth's grounding presence for a draught that encourages you to stand up for your truths.

ice cubes

40 ml (1¼ oz) whisky

30 ml (1 oz) Cynar

30 ml (1 oz) sweet vermouth

orange twist, to garnish

Fill a mixing glass with ice and pour in the whisky, Cynar and vermouth. Stir briskly, then strain into a chilled cocktail glass.

Garnish with the orange twist.

COURAGE'S FORGE

In ancient times, sprigs of fragrant thyme were carried to impart courage and energy. Here, a syrup made with the herb lends a fragrant note to bourbon and bitters for a spell that can help conjure courage and help you face tasks head on. Drink in the last light of the setting sun for a jolt of complementary solar energy.

ice cubes, plus 1 large ice cube

60 ml (2 oz) bourbon

3 dashes Angostura bitters

20 ml (¾ oz) Thyme syrup (page 130)

thyme sprig, to garnish

orange wedge, to garnish

Fill a mixing glass with ice and add in the bourbon, Angostura bitters and thyme syrup. Stir briskly.

Place the large ice cube in a tumbler and strain in the drink. Garnish with the sprig of thyme and orange wedge.

VISION

To focus the mind.
To cultivate self-knowledge.
To enhance intuition. To encourage wisdom.
To channel psychic dreams.
To embrace clarity. To stimulate creativity.
To experience revelation.
To receive the wisdom
of the universe.

Vision helps us to see things clearly
and connect with our innermost self.

Encourage vision through attention
to the ebb and flow of energy;
the natural cycles of life; and the
ever-changing seasons.

Open your mind's eye.

SERVES 1

SPICED DIVINATION

Witches have long used branches from the almond tree as divining rods used to uncover hidden treasures, the nuts themselves associated with mystical wisdom. This recipe blends almond milk with warming spices, amaretto and a dash of coffee for a drink that clears the mind and enhances inner vision.

45 ml (1½ oz) almond milk

¼ teaspoon ground allspice, plus extra to garnish

¼ teaspoon ground cardamom

¼ teaspoon ground nutmeg

ice cubes

30 ml (1 oz) amaretto

15 ml (½ oz) coffee liqueur

15 ml (½ oz) Vanilla syrup (page 131)

Combine the almond milk, allspice, cardamom and nutmeg in a small saucepan and bring to a simmer. Reduce the heat to low, whisking constantly until the spices are well dispersed. Allow to cool.

Fill a cocktail shaker with ice and add the spiced almond milk, amaretto, coffee liqueur and vanilla syrup. Shake well for 30 seconds.

Strain into a tumbler filled with ice. Garnish with an extra sprinkling of allspice.

SAGE'S SIPPER

Sage is known to enhance wisdom, an attribute that can be deepened by pairing it with honey. The corn in the bourbon mingles here with the two to lend a touch of divinatory power. To enjoy this drink's rich flavours at their most potent, focus on Athena or another goddess of wisdom as you slowly sip.

6 sage leaves

45 ml (1½ oz) bourbon

30 ml (1 oz) sweet vermouth

5 ml (¼ oz) Honey syrup (page 128)

30 ml (1 oz) orange juice

ice cubes

Place five of the sage leaves in a cocktail shaker with the bourbon, vermouth and honey syrup. Gently crush the leaves with a muddling tool, then add the orange juice and ice. Shake well for 30 seconds.

Strain into a tumbler and garnish with the remaining sage leaf.

MIND'S EYE

According to lore, mulberry is the wisest of trees, because it is late in unfolding its leaves, and so escapes the dangerous frosts of early spring. The fruit has long been used by magical practitioners to enhance wisdom and improve psychic awareness. Whenever you wish to open your mind's eye and receive the universe's wisdom, use the berry to create this elixir.

ice cubes

60 ml (2 oz) Mulberry gin (page 122)

30 ml (1 oz) lemon juice

15 ml (½ oz) Honey syrup (page 128)

3 dashes orange bitters

3 mulberries, to garnish

Fill a cocktail shaker with ice and add the mulberry gin, lemon juice, honey syrup and orange bitters. Shake well for 30 seconds.

Strain into a tumbler filled with ice and garnish with the mulberries.

SCRYING GLASS FIZZ

This effervescent drink opens the mind to revelations, drawing on the magical properties of peach and wine to usher in self-knowledge and inner wisdom. The mint helps cleanse the way and sharpens your psychic senses. Try consuming this fizz before working with divination, and prepare on a Monday so the Moon can heighten its effects.

8 mint leaves
180 ml (6 oz) rosé
60 ml (2 oz) peach nectar
5 ml (¼ oz) lemon juice
ice cubes, plus crushed ice
chilled sparkling water, to top
peach wedge, to garnish

Place five of the mint leaves in a cocktail shaker and pour in the rosé, peach nectar and lemon juice. Gently crush the leaves with a muddling tool, then add ice. Shake well for 30 seconds.

Strain into a large, chilled wine glass filled with ice and top up with sparkling water. Garnish with the remaining mint leaves and the peach wedge.

SERVES 1

DRAGON'S DRAM

Looking to enhance your creativity? Try combining dragon fruit and pineapple-infused rum with lime. Their fiery energies can help stimulate the imagination and assist with turning idle dreams into reality, while the sugar is a great tool to attract your desires. Mix this drink up when you are seeking a creative solution to a problem or want to infuse a project with energy.

1 dragon fruit

ice cubes

60 ml (2 oz) Pineapple rum (page 124)

20 ml (¾ oz) lime juice

5 ml (¼ oz) Simple syrup (page 128)

pineapple wedge, to garnish

Peel the dragon fruit, slice off a wedge and set aside. Cut the remaining dragon fruit into chunks and puree in a blender, adding a splash of water if needed to loosen the fruit up.

Fill a cocktail shaker with ice and add the pineapple rum, lime juice, simple syrup and 20 ml (¾ oz) of the puree. Shake vigorously for 30 seconds.

Strain into a chilled cocktail glass. Garnish with the reserved dragon fruit and the pineapple wedge.

TINCTURE OF CLARITY

Celery is associated with psychic awareness and mental powers – legend has it that witches in ancient times would consume its seeds before mounting brooms so they wouldn't become dizzy and fall. Enjoy its powers through this intriguing cocktail for a clarifying effect.

1 teaspoon celery salt

1 lemon wedge

ice cubes, plus crushed ice

40 ml (1¼ oz) mezcal

20 ml (¾ oz) lime juice

20 ml (¾ oz) Honey syrup (page 128)

2–3 drops celery bitters

10 ml (¼ oz) celery juice

Place the celery salt on a small plate. Run the lemon wedge around the rim of a chilled cocktail glass, then dip the rim of the glass in the celery salt to coat.

Fill a cocktail shaker with ice and add the mezcal, lime juice, honey syrup and celery bitters. Shake well for 30 seconds.

Fill the cocktail glass with crushed ice and strain in the drink. Finish with the celery juice.

SERVES 1

PROPHECY'S SCENT

Jasmine, with its heady fragrance, is favoured for invoking prophetic dreams. To harness and strengthen this gift, dried blossoms are combined with crisp, dry gin and citrus in this draught. Prepare under the full moon to best tap into your powers of foresight.

5 g (¼ oz) jasmine tea leaves

125 ml (4 oz) near-boiling water

50 ml (1¾ oz) dry gin

25 ml (¾ oz) orange liqueur

10 ml (¼ oz) lemon juice

10 ml (¼ oz) Simple syrup (page 128)

15 ml (½ oz) egg white

ice cubes

lemon twist, to garnish

Steep the tea leaves in the hot water for 3–4 minutes, depending on how strong you like your tea. Strain the tea and refrigerate until cold.

Pour the gin, orange liqueur, lemon juice, simple syrup, egg white and 10 ml (¼ oz) of the jasmine tea into a cocktail shaker and dry shake for 15 seconds. Add ice and shake for a further 15 seconds.

Strain into a chilled cocktail glass and garnish with the lemon twist.

SAMHAIN MARTINI

Pomegranate is considered a lucky fruit, its seeds used as a tool in divination. Here, it is paired with triple sec's oranges, which allow you to pull from the well of creativity. Vodka adds a touch of clarity, sake a watery energy. Prepare at Samhain, when the veil between the physical and spirit worlds thins, to embrace this period of exploration and communion.

ice cubes

30 ml (1 oz) sake

15 ml (½ oz) vodka

15 ml (½ oz) triple sec

30 ml (1 oz) pomegranate juice

10 ml (¼ oz) lemon juice

15 ml (½ oz) Simple syrup (page 128)

2–3 drops orange bitters

pomegranate seeds, to garnish

Fill a cocktail shaker with ice and add the sake, vodka, triple sec, pomegranate juice, lemon juice, simple syrup and orange bitters. Shake well for 30 seconds.

Strain into a chilled martini glass and garnish with pomegranate seeds.

FRUIT OF FORESIGHT

Cherries are used to divine the future – here, infused gin combines the fruit with the marzipan-like aroma of amaretto for a drink that stimulates intuition and helps you see the best way forward: particularly in relationships, as cherries are the dominion of Venus.

ice cubes, plus 1 large ice cube

30 ml (1 oz) Cherry gin (page 124) or cherry brandy

20 ml (¾ oz) Campari

20 ml (¾ oz) sweet vermouth

15 ml (½ oz) amaretto

2–3 drops orange bitters

maraschino cherry, to garnish

orange twist, to garnish

Fill a mixing glass with ice and pour in the cherry gin, Campari, vermouth, amaretto and orange bitters. Stir briskly.

Place the large ice cube in a tumbler and strain in the drink. Garnish with the maraschino cherry and orange twist.

WAKING MARTINI

The hazel tree has old associations with wisdom and enhancing mental abilities, while coffee beans have an invigorating effect on the intellect and spirit. This delicious take on the espresso martini is the perfect drink for anyone wishing to stimulate the conscious mind and strengthen their mental powers.

ice cubes

40 ml (1¼ oz) vodka

30 ml (1 oz) chilled espresso

15 ml (½ oz) coffee liqueur

10 ml (¼ oz) hazelnut liqueur

10 ml (¼ oz) Simple syrup (page 128)

3 coffee beans, to garnish

Fill a cocktail shaker with ice and add the vodka, espresso, coffee liqueur, hazelnut liqueur and simple syrup. Shake vigorously for 15 seconds.

Strain into a chilled martini glass and garnish with the coffee beans.

LUCK

To cultivate good fortune.
To usher in changes.
To welcome abundance.
To attract happiness. To invite opportunities.
To foster positivity. To create the chance.
To set you on your truest path.

Luck is a spark that can be cultivated
through intention. It's a practice of noticing
and receiving the bounty of
the universe.

What if the things you wish for
were already so?

Luck be with you!

HARVEST

This recipe calls for corn liqueur, a unique spirit that draws on the crop's association with luck and abundance. Symbolising a harvest ready to be reaped, this drink welcomes destiny to flourish at just the right time, the lime juice helping to ensure it's a happy bounty.

1 teaspoon salt

1 lime wedge

ice cubes

45 ml (1½ oz) mezcal

30 ml (1 oz) Nixta corn liqueur

30 ml (1 oz) agave syrup

15 ml (½ oz) lime juice

Place the salt on a small plate. Run the lime wedge around the rim of a chilled tumbler, then dip the rim of the tumbler in the salt to coat.

Fill a cocktail shaker with ice and add the mezcal, corn liqueur, agave syrup and lime juice. Shake well for 30 seconds.

Fill the tumbler with ice and strain in the drink.

FORTUNA

Oranges have long symbolised luck and good fortune, in part due to the tree's rare ability to produce fruit, flowers and foliage simultaneously. Sugar's powers of attraction weave through the fruit's properties to finish this bright elixir. Call upon Tyche or another goddess of fortune if you'd like to fortify the effects.

ice cubes

45 ml (1½ oz) cognac or brandy

30 ml (1 oz) triple sec

30 ml (1 oz) lemon juice

10 ml (¼ oz) orange juice

5 ml (¼ oz) Simple syrup (page 128)

orange twist, to garnish

Fill a cocktail shaker with ice and add the cognac, triple sec, lemon juice, orange juice and simple syrup. Shake well for 30 seconds, then strain into a chilled cocktail glass.

Garnish with the orange twist.

MIDSUMMER SPRITZ

Among basil's gifts, it is thought to aid in success. Its herbaceous addition to this refreshing spritz evokes Mars, while sweet limoncello and fresh lemon juice call upon the Sun. Combined, these energies make for an invigorating combination that brings positive luck. Best drunk on Thursday, to invite Jupiter's fortuitous presence.

7 basil leaves, plus sprig to garnish

60 ml (2 oz) limoncello

30 ml (1 oz) vodka

15 ml (½ oz) lemon juice

15 ml (½ oz) Simple syrup (page 128)

ice cubes and crushed ice

chilled sparkling water, to top

Place seven of the basil leaves in a cocktail shaker with the limoncello, vodka, lemon juice and simple syrup. Gently crush the leaves with a muddling tool, then add ice. Shake well for 30 seconds.

Strain into a large, chilled wine glass filled with ice. Top up with sparkling water and garnish with the basil sprig.

SERVES 1

GARDEN OF DELIGHT

This fragrant, subtle drink calls on the pear, which is symbolic of abundance and inspires happiness. The fizz of the sparkling wine imparts a burst of energy, carrying with it chamomile's lucky scent, for a creation that is perfect to prepare when you'd like to welcome good tidings into your coven.

250 ml (8½ oz) Chamomile gin (page 126)

80 ml (2½ oz) pear liqueur

60 ml (2 oz) Simple syrup (page 128)

60 ml (2 oz) lemon juice

1 bottle chilled sparkling wine

ice cubes

12 edible chamomile flowers, to garnish

Pour the chamomile gin, pear liqueur, simple syrup and lemon juice into a jug and stir to combine.

Divide among six cocktail glasses and top each with sparkling wine. Add an ice cube and garnish each drink with two chamomile flowers.

SERVES 1

THE INVITATION

Witches have favoured honeysuckle for many years, its sweet scent signifying the joy of life and good fortune. This effervescent drink is best enjoyed at twilight, when the scent of honeysuckle flowers is at its strongest, to take advantage of their most potent magical effects.

ice cubes

60 ml (2 oz) vodka

15 ml (½ oz) lemon juice

30 ml (1 oz) Honeysuckle syrup (page 131)

chilled sparkling wine, to top

edible honeysuckle flower, to garnish

Fill a cocktail shaker with ice and add the vodka, lemon juice and honeysuckle syrup. Shake well for 30 seconds, then strain into a chilled champagne flute.

Top up with sparkling wine and garnish with the honeysuckle.

HIGH SUN

The marigold, with its bright clusters of petals, radiates with power of the Sun. In a spell, this energy can be invoked for joy and abundance: an attribute shared by oranges, which are mixed into this margarita for an even stronger burst of sunshine. For best results, use marigolds that have been picked at noon, when the Sun is strongest.

1 teaspoon salt

1 teaspoon dried edible marigold petals

lime wedge

ice cubes

45 ml (1½ oz) tequila

30 ml (1 oz) triple sec

30 ml (1 oz) orange juice

15 ml (½ oz) lime juice

25 ml (¾ oz) Marigold syrup (page 132)

fresh edible marigold flower, to garnish

Mix the salt and dried marigold petals together on a small plate. Run the lime wedge around the rim of a chilled tumbler, then dip the rim of the glass in the marigold salt. Set aside.

Fill a cocktail shaker with ice and add the tequila, triple sec, orange juice, lime juice and marigold syrup. Shake well for 30 seconds.

Fill the tumbler with ice and strain in the drink. Garnish with the marigold.

LIQUID LUCK

Strawberries, a fruit of fortune, are used to create creme de fraise des bois. Meanwhile rum is made with sugarcane which, like the berry, has a watery energy. While this element can be slow-moving in its effects, its steady flow can fill our cup until it's overflowing. Call upon it through this drink on a Sunday to invite an even stronger flow of happiness.

4 strawberries, hulled

45 ml (1½ oz) white rum

45 ml (1½ oz) creme de fraise des bois

15 ml (½ oz) Simple syrup (page 128)

ice cubes

Halve three of the strawberries and place them in a cocktail shaker. Add the white rum, creme de fraise des bois and simple syrup. Gently crush the strawberries with a muddling tool, then add ice and shake well for 30 seconds.

Strain into a chilled coupe glass and garnish with the remaining strawberry.

INVOCATION

This rich, layered creation calls upon the forest's hazel and oak trees and the field's swathes of corn to inspire happiness. The corn, which is present in bourbon, is symbolic of fertility. Stirred together with the ancient luck and protection of the trees, its powers work to help dreams flourish, hazel's touch of wisdom guiding you on your path.

ice cubes, plus 1 large ice cube

60 ml (2 oz) bourbon

25 ml (¾ oz) hazelnut liqueur

15 ml (½ oz) maple syrup

3 dashes oak bitters

orange peel, to garnish

Fill a mixing glass with ice and add the bourbon, hazelnut liqueur, maple syrup and oak bitters. Stir briskly.

Place the ice cube into a tumbler and strain in the drink. Garnish with the orange peel.

PERSEPHONE'S BREATH

Combining an abundance-boosting touch of oranges with pomegranate's fortune-enhancing qualities, this concoction is suited to opening the door to renewal and joy. The rum's spices add energy to these effects, from the heat of the cinnamon to the luck of the allspice and star anise. Prepare as an offering to Persephone to inspire a personal blossoming.

ice cubes

45 ml (1½ oz) Spiced rum (page 125)

15 ml (½ oz) triple sec

30 ml (1 oz) orange juice

20 ml (¾ oz) pomegranate juice

pomegranate seeds, to garnish

star anise, to garnish

cinnamon stick, to garnish

Fill a mixing glass with ice and pour in the spiced rum, triple sec, orange juice and pomegranate juice. Stir briskly.

Strain into a tumbler filled with ice and garnish with the pomegranate seeds, star anise and cinnamon stick.

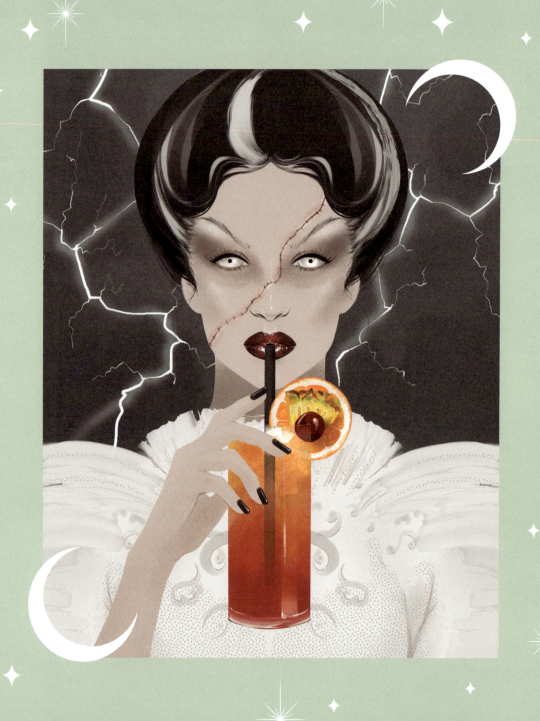

SERVES 1

LUCKY ZOMBIE

Brimming with tropical flavours, this classic cocktail helps the drinker embrace change and stay open to opportunities. Created with a cornucopia of luck-inspiring and purifying ingredients, this creation represents life's bounty – drink deeply and will your chosen future into being.

ice cubes

30 ml (1 oz) white rum

30 ml (1 oz) gold rum

30 ml (1 oz) dark rum

15 ml (½ oz) falernum liqueur

5 ml (¼ oz) anise liqueur

5 ml (¼ oz) Cinnamon syrup (page 132)

30 ml (1 oz) pineapple juice

15 ml (½ oz) lime juice

15 ml (½ oz) grapefruit juice

2–3 drops orange bitters

5 ml (¼ oz) grenadine

maraschino cherry, to garnish

pineapple wedge, to garnish

orange slice, to garnish

Fill a cocktail shaker with ice and add all the ingredients, except the grenadine. Shake well for 30 seconds, then strain into a tall, chilled glass filled with ice.

Drizzle the grenadine on top. Garnish with the cherry, pineapple wedge and orange slice.

HARMONY

To connect with the energy of all things.
To bring light and dark into balance.
To calm the mind.
To ward off negative influences.
To deepen your connection with the Earth.
To go gently. To find inner peace.
To rest easy.
To listen to your heart's song.

Harmony exists within you.
Even when you are surrounded by chaos,
an inner reservoir of peace and tranquillity
is always available, waiting for you to
tap into its still waters.

Attune yourself to this harmony
and find your equilibrium.

Peace in all things.

RHEA'S TOUCH

A chamomile-infused gin forms the basis of this soothing cocktail, imbuing it with the flower's calming properties. Honey, meanwhile, adds the sweetness of summer; associated with Rhea, the Greek goddess of, among many things, comfort, the amber liquid fortifies this spell, making it ideal for anyone looking to connect to nature's grounding essence.

ice cubes

60 ml (2 oz) Chamomile gin (page 126)

15 ml (½ oz) lemon juice

20 ml (¾ oz) Honey syrup (page 128)

edible chamomile flower, to garnish

Fill a cocktail shaker with ice and add the chamomile gin, lemon juice and honey syrup. Shake well for 30 seconds and strain into a chilled martini glass.

Garnish with the chamomile flower.

SWEET HARMONY

The apricot imparts both a sweetness to the heart and peace to the soul – for this reason, it is equally suited to rituals of harmony and rituals of love. Here, the fruit is paired with gin and honey for a libation that helps you embrace your potential and find the sweetness of life, the energy of the sparkling wine adding an uplifting finish.

ice cubes

60 ml (2 oz) gin

10 ml (¼ oz) apricot brandy

25 ml (¾ oz) lemon juice

15 ml (½ oz) Honey syrup (page 128)

chilled sparkling wine, to top

apricot wedge on a cocktail stick, to garnish

Fill a cocktail shaker with ice and add the gin, apricot brandy, lemon juice and honey syrup. Shake well for 30 seconds, then strain into a chilled coupe glass.

Top up with sparkling wine and garnish with the apricot wedge on the cocktail stick.

TRANQUIL WATERS

Cucumber is thought to have restorative qualities, while lavender has been used since the ancient world to soothe the mind. This elixir combines these two ingredients with the calming and transformative butterfly pea flower for a draught that helps you find peace, even in times of confusion.

1 short cucumber, peeled and roughly chopped

60 ml (2 oz) Butterfly pea gin (page 122)

20 ml (¾ oz) Lavender syrup (page 129)

crushed ice

edible lavender sprig, to garnish

Put the cucumber in a blender and blitz into a fine mixture. Pass the mixture through a muslin-lined strainer into a small bowl, discarding the solids.

Pour 60 ml (2 oz) of the cucumber juice into a tumbler. Add the butterfly pea gin and lavender syrup and stir to combine. Top up with crushed ice and garnish with the lavender sprig.

CLEANSING FIZZ

Sloe gin – made from blackthorn fruit – carries within it potent protective powers, as does plum, while lemon purifies. Combined, they offer a drink that both wards off and cleanses negative influences to guard inner calm. For even more protection, mix this tincture on a Saturday to capture Saturn's power.

½ plum

50 ml (1¾ oz) Sloe gin (page 123)

25 ml (¾ oz) lemon juice

10 ml (¼ oz) Simple syrup (page 128)

ice cubes

chilled sparkling water, to top

lemon wheel, to garnish

Place the plum in a cocktail shaker and add the sloe gin, lemon juice and simple syrup. Gently muddle the plum with a muddling tool, then add ice and shake well for 30 seconds.

Strain into a tall, chilled glass filled with ice. Top up with sparkling water and garnish with the lemon wheel.

COVEN'S WARD

Mint refreshes the mind and revitalises the spirit with its sharp scent. This drink uses the fresh herb, as well as creme de menthe, to impart its invigorating effect while also taking advantage of its ability to ward off evil and offer protection – an effect that gin's juniper amplifies.

10 mint leaves, plus extra mint leaf to garnish

45 ml (1½ oz) dry gin

30 ml (1 oz) dry white wine

10 ml (¼ oz) creme de menthe

10 ml (¼ oz) Simple syrup (page 128)

ice cubes

Place the 10 mint leaves in a cocktail shaker and add the gin, white wine, creme de menthe and simple syrup. Gently crush the leaves with a muddling tool, add ice and shake well for 30 seconds.

Strain into a chilled coupe glass and garnish with the remaining mint leaf.

AS ABOVE, SO BELOW

Apples have deep ties to the mystical; associated with many gods, they are symbolic of both immortality and the soul and are viewed as a powerful tool in magic. Here, warming cinnamon combines with the fruit to form a soothing brew that helps put all things in balance, drawing on the apple's properties of healing and harmony.

½ teaspoon ground cinnamon

15 g (½ oz) caster (superfine) sugar

1 lemon wedge

ice cubes

40 ml (1¼ oz) Cinnamon & apple whisky (page 127)

20 ml (¾ oz) vodka

chilled sweet apple cider, to top

¼ red apple, thinly sliced, to garnish

Mix the cinnamon and sugar together on a small plate. Run the lemon wedge around the rim of a tall, chilled glass, then dip the rim of the glass in the cinnamon sugar to coat.

Fill the glass with ice. Pour in the whisky and vodka and stir to combine. Top up with cider and garnish with the apple slices.

SERVES 1

HEX BREAKER

The complex notes of absinthe are produced with purifying fennel and protective wormwood and anise. These combine with St-Germain's elderflowers, which have long been celebrated for their powerful ability to ward off evil spirits. Herbal, floral and aromatic, this spell can help shield the drinker from ill will and bewitchment.

ice cubes

20 ml (¾ oz) dry gin

20 ml (¾ oz) St-Germain

20 ml (¾ oz) Lillet Blanc

dash of absinthe

20 ml (¾ oz) lemon juice

lemon twist, to garnish

Fill a cocktail shaker with ice and pour in the gin, St-Germain, Lillet Blanc, absinthe and lemon juice. Shake for 30 seconds, then strain into a chilled coupe glass.

Garnish with the lemon twist.

SERENITY'S HATCHING

From the egg, many things are birthed; among these are protection and cleansing, which are amplified by the fruit distilled into this cocktail's liquors. The grapefruit, lemon and blackberry all further these effects, making for a serenity-inducing sip. Prepare under the new moon to welcome a fresh start.

30 ml (1 oz) dry gin

30 ml (1 oz) Sloe gin (page 123)

10 ml (¼ oz) Chambord

30 ml (1 oz) pink grapefruit juice

10 ml (¼ oz) lemon juice

5 ml (¼ oz) Simple syrup (page 128)

15 ml (½ oz) egg white

lemon twist, to garnish

blackberry, to garnish

Add the gin, sloe gin, Chambord, grapefruit juice, lemon juice, simple syrup and egg white to a cocktail shaker and dry shake for 15 seconds. Add ice and shake for a further 15 seconds.

Strain into a chilled cocktail glass and garnish with the lemon twist and blackberry.

GARDEN CHARM

A purifying touch of grapefruit with a protective sprig of rosemary and a drop of elderflower create this tart, herbaceous cocktail. Working together, the magic of these plants can help you ward off negative energies and be your own best protector. Keep Harmonia or another goddess of peace in mind for extra power.

ice cubes

60 ml (2 oz) vodka

30 ml (1 oz) St-Germain

30 ml (1 oz) pink grapefruit juice

10 ml (¼ oz) Rosemary syrup (page 130)

3 dashes grapefruit bitters

rosemary sprig, to garnish

grapefruit slice, to garnish

Fill a mixing glass with ice and add the vodka, St-Germain, grapefruit juice, rosemary syrup and grapefruit bitters. Stir briskly, then strain into a chilled cocktail glass.

Garnish with the rosemary sprig and grapefruit slice.

GRIMOIRE GIMLET

The evergreen leaves of rosemary possess the ability to promote harmony. The herb pairs perfectly with the botanical character of gin, which contains juniper – a tree known for its protective qualities. This twist on the classic gimlet has a refreshing, herbaceous character, with a stabilising and balancing effect.

ice cubes

60 ml (2 oz) gin

30 ml (1 oz) lime juice

15 ml (½ oz) Rosemary syrup (page 130)

rosemary sprig, to garnish

Fill a cocktail shaker with ice and add the gin, lime juice and rosemary syrup. Shake well for 30 seconds, then strain into a chilled coupe glass.

Garnish with the rosemary sprig.

INFUSIONS

& SYRUPS

BUTTERFLY PEA GIN

Makes 750 ml (3 cups)

4–6 washed lavender sprigs, flowers picked and stems discarded

1 tablespoon dried edible butterfly pea flowers

750 ml (3 cups) gin

Place the lavender flowers in a 1 litre (4 cup) capacity clean jar or container with a lid (see page 9). Add the butterfly pea flowers and gin, then cover with the lid and shake gently.

Leave to infuse for 2–3 hours, then taste the infusion to check if you are happy with the flavour, leaving for longer if you want a stronger flavour.

Pass the gin through a muslin-lined strainer into a jug, discarding the solids. Transfer to a clean jar or container, seal and use as desired.

MULBERRY GIN

Makes 750 ml (3 cups)

550 g (1 lb 3 oz) mulberries

750 ml (3 cups) gin

115 g (½ cup) caster (superfine) sugar

Place the mulberries in a clean 1 litre (4 cup) capacity jar or container with a lid (see page 9) and muddle them. Add the gin and sugar, ensuring the fruit is fully submerged. Cover with the lid and shake gently.

Leave in a cool, dark place for 1 week, gently shaking each day. Taste the infusion to check if you are happy with the flavour, leaving for longer if you want a stronger flavour.

Pass the gin through a muslin-lined strainer into a jug, discarding the solids. Transfer to a clean jar or container, seal and use as desired.

CONCOCTIONS

SLOE GIN

Makes 750 ml (3 cups)

500 g (1 lb 2 oz) sloe berries

750 ml (3 cups) gin

215 g (7 1/2 oz) caster (superfine) sugar

Place the sloe berries in a clean 1 litre (4 cup) capacity jar or container with a lid (see page 9). Gently muddle the berries, then add the gin and sugar, ensuring the fruit is fully submerged. Cover with the lid and shake gently.

Leave in a cool, dark place for 3 months, gently shaking every other day. Taste the infusion to check if you are happy with the flavour, leaving for longer if you want a stronger flavour.

Pass the sloe gin through a muslin-lined strainer into a jug, discarding the solids. Transfer to a clean jar or container, seal and use as desired.

CHERRY GIN

Makes 750 ml (3 cups)

450 g (1 lb) cherries, pitted and quartered

750 ml (3 cups) gin

115 g (½ cup) caster (superfine) sugar

Place the cherries in a clean 1 litre (4 cup) capacity jar or container with a lid (see page 9) and muddle them. Add the gin and sugar, ensuring the fruit is fully submerged. Cover with the lid and shake gently.

Leave in a cool, dark place for 1 week, gently shaking each day. Taste the infusion to check if you are happy with the flavour, leaving for longer if you want a stronger flavour.

Pass the gin through a muslin-lined strainer into a jug, discarding the solids. Transfer to a clean jar or container, seal and use as desired.

PINEAPPLE RUM

Makes 750 ml (3 cups)

1 pineapple, peeled and diced

750 ml (3 cups) white or gold rum

Place the pineapple in a clean 1 litre (4 cup) capacity jar or container with a lid (see page 9). Pour in the rum, covering the pineapple completely. Cover with the lid and shake gently.

Leave in a cool, dark place, gently shaking and tasting the infusion every 1–2 days for up to 1 week until you are happy with the flavour.

Pass the rum through a muslin-lined strainer into a jug, discarding the solids. Transfer to a clean jar or container, seal and use as desired.

SPICED RUM

Makes 750 ml (3 cups)

750 ml (3 cups) white or gold rum

3 allspice berries

4 black peppercorns

¼ teaspoon grated nutmeg

1 cinnamon stick

2 star anise

10 cm (4 in) strip orange peel, pith removed

2.5 cm (1 in) piece ginger, peeled and thinly sliced

3 cloves

1 vanilla bean, split lengthways and seeds scraped

Place all the ingredients in a clean 1 litre (4 cup) capacity jar or container with a lid (see page 9). Cover with the lid and shake gently.

Leave in a cool, dark place for 1 week, gently shaking each day. Taste the infusion to check if you are happy with the flavour, leaving for longer if you want a stronger flavour.

Pass the rum through a muslin-lined strainer into a jug, discarding the solids. Transfer to a clean jar or container, seal and use as desired.

INFUSIONS

GINGER TEQUILA

Makes 750 ml (3 cups)

2 large pieces of ginger, peeled and thinly sliced

750 ml (3 cups) tequila blanco

Place the ginger and tequila in a clean 1 litre (4 cup) capacity jar or container with a lid (see page 9). Cover with the lid and shake gently.

Leave in a cool, dark place for 5–7 days, gently shaking and tasting the infusion each day until you are happy with the flavour.

Pass the tequila through a muslin-lined strainer into a jug, discarding the solids. Transfer to a clean jar or container, seal and use as desired.

CHAMOMILE GIN

Makes 750 ml (3 cups)

½ cup dried edible chamomile flowers

750 ml (3 cups) gin

Place the flowers and gin in a clean 1 litre (4 cup) capacity jar or container with a lid (see page 9). Cover with the lid and shake gently.

Leave in a cool, dark place for 1–2 days. Taste the infusion to check if you are happy with the flavour, leaving for longer if you want a stronger flavour.

Pass the gin through a muslin-lined strainer into a jug, discarding the solids. Transfer to a clean jar or container, seal and use as desired.

CINNAMON & APPLE WHISKY

Makes 750 ml (3 cups)

2 red apples, cored and thinly sliced

750 ml (3 cups) whisky

5 cinnamon sticks

Place the apple in a clean 1 litre (4 cup) capacity jar or container with a lid (see page 9). Pour in the whisky, ensuring the apples are fully covered. Cover with the lid and gently shake.

Leave in a cool, dark place. After 3 days, add the cinnamon sticks, close the jar and gently shake. Return the jar to the dark place for a further 3–4 days, tasting daily until you are happy with the flavour.

Pass the whisky through a muslin-lined strainer into a jug, discarding the solids. Transfer to a clean jar or container, seal and use as desired.

INFUSIONS

SIMPLE SYRUP

Makes 55 ml (1¾ oz)

55 g (¼ cup) caster (superfine) sugar

Combine the sugar and 60 ml (¼ cup) of water in a small saucepan. Bring to the boil and stir until the sugar has dissolved. Remove from the heat and allow to cool.

The simple syrup will keep in an airtight container in the fridge for up to 1 week.

HONEY SYRUP

Makes 125 ml (½ cup)

90 g (¼ cup) honey

Combine the honey and 90 ml (3 oz) of water in a small saucepan over low heat. Stir until the honey has dissolved. Remove from the heat and allow to cool.

The honey syrup will keep in an airtight container in the fridge for up to 1 week.

ROSE SYRUP

Makes 125 ml (½ cup)

½ cup dried edible rose petals

115 g (½ cup) caster (superfine) sugar

Combine the rose petals, sugar and 125 ml (½ cup) of water in a small saucepan. Bring to the boil and stir until the sugar has dissolved. Remove from the heat and allow to cool, then refrigerate for 4 hours, or overnight for a stronger flavour. Strain through a fine-mesh sieve into a container, discarding the solids.

The rose petal syrup will keep in an airtight container in the fridge for 4–5 days.

LAVENDER SYRUP

Makes 55 ml (1¾ oz)

2–3 teaspoons dried edible lavender flowers

55 g (¼ cup) caster (superfine) sugar

Combine 2 teaspoons of the dried lavender, the sugar and 60 ml (¼ cup) of water in a small saucepan – add an extra teaspoon of lavender if you would like a stronger flavour. Bring to the boil and stir until the sugar has dissolved. Remove from the heat and leave to infuse for 30 minutes. Strain through a muslin-lined sieve into a container, discarding the solids.

The lavender syrup will keep in an airtight container in the fridge for 4–5 days.

ROSEMARY SYRUP

Makes 55 ml (1¾ oz)

2 rosemary sprigs, leaves picked and roughly chopped, stems discarded

55 g (¼ cup) caster (superfine) sugar

Combine the rosemary, sugar and 60 ml (¼ cup) of water in a small saucepan. Bring to the boil and stir until the sugar has dissolved. Remove from the heat and leave to infuse for 30 minutes. Strain through a fine-mesh sieve into a container, discarding the solids.

The rosemary syrup will keep in an airtight container in the fridge for 4–5 days.

THYME SYRUP

Makes 55 ml (1¾ oz)

4 thyme sprigs

55 g (1/4 cup) caster (superfine) sugar

Combine the thyme, sugar and 60 ml (¼ cup) of water in a small saucepan. Bring to the boil and stir until the sugar has dissolved. Remove from the heat and leave to infuse for 30 minutes. Strain through a fine-mesh sieve into a container, discarding the solids.

The thyme syrup will keep in an airtight container in the fridge for 4–5 days.

HONEYSUCKLE SYRUP

Makes 205–235 ml (7–8 oz)

1 cup edible honeysuckle petals, green parts and leaves removed

250 ml (1 cup) near-boiling water

170–230 g (¾–1 cup) caster (superfine) sugar

Combine the honeysuckle and water in a heatproof container. Stir well, then cover and leave to infuse in the fridge overnight.

Pass the mixture through a fine mesh strainer into a measuring jug, discarding the solids. Add an equal measure of sugar, then transfer to a small saucepan. Bring to the boil and stir until the sugar has dissolved. Remove from the heat and allow to cool.

The honeysuckle syrup will keep in an airtight container in the fridge for 4–5 days.

VANILLA SYRUP

Makes 125 ml (½ cup)

1 vanilla bean, split lengthways and seeds scraped

110 g (4 oz) caster (superfine) sugar

Combine the vanilla bean and seeds, sugar and 125 ml (½ cup) of water in a saucepan. Bring to the boil and stir until the sugar has dissolved. Remove from the heat and allow to cool, then strain through a muslin-lined sieve into a container, discarding the solids.

The vanilla syrup will keep in an airtight container in the fridge for 4–5 days.

SYRUPS

MARIGOLD SYRUP

Makes 55 ml (1¾ oz)

1 tablespoon dried edible
marigold petals

55 g (¼ cup) caster (superfine)
sugar

Combine the marigold petals, sugar and 60 ml (¼ cup) of water in a small saucepan. Bring to the boil and stir until the sugar has dissolved. Remove from the heat and leave to infuse for 30 minutes. Strain through a muslin-lined sieve into a container, discarding the solids.

The marigold syrup will keep in an airtight container in the fridge for 4–5 days.

CINNAMON SYRUP

Makes 55 ml (1¾ oz)

1 cinnamon stick

55 g (¼ cup) caster (superfine)
sugar

Lightly crush the cinnamon into pieces using a mortar and pestle. Transfer to a small saucepan along with the sugar and 60 ml (¼ cup) of water. Bring to a boil, stirring until the sugar has dissolved. Remove from the heat and leave to infuse for 2 hours. Strain through a muslin-lined sieve into a container, discarding the solids.

The cinnamon syrup will keep in an airtight container in the fridge for 4–5 days.

CHAI SYRUP

Makes 125 ml (½ cup)

1 cinnamon stick

5 cloves

3 cardamon pods

5 black peppercorns

¼ teaspoon grated nutmeg

1 vanilla bean, split lengthways and seeds scraped

1 cm (½ in) piece of ginger, peeled and sliced

110 g (4 oz) brown sugar

Lightly crush the cinnamon, cloves, cardamon and peppercorns using a mortar and pestle. Transfer to a small saucepan along with the remaining ingredients and 125 ml (½ cup) of water. Bring to a boil, stirring until the sugar has dissolved. Remove from the heat and leave to infuse for 2 hours. Strain through a muslin-lined sieve into a container, discarding the solids.

The chai syrup will keep in an airtight container in the fridge for 4–5 days.

SAFFRON SYRUP

Makes 55 ml (1¾ oz)

5 saffron threads

55 g (¼ cup) caster (superfine) sugar

Combine the saffron, sugar and 60 ml (¼ cup) of water in a saucepan. Bring to the boil and stir until the sugar has dissolved. Remove from the heat and allow to cool, then strain through a muslin-lined sieve into a container, discarding the solids.

The saffron syrup will keep in an airtight container in the fridge for 4–5 days.

INDEX

A

absinthe, Hex breaker 112
Alignment 46
amaretto
    Fruit of foresight 72
    Spiced divination 56
anise liqueur, Lucky
    zombie 97
apricot brandy, Sweet
    harmony 103
apricot liqueur,
    Transfixer 15
As above, so below 111

B

bitters
    Courage's forge 53
    Duality 16
    Fruit of foresight 72
    Garden Charm 116
    Inner ward 37
    Lucky zombie 97
    Mind's eye 60
    Samhain martini 71
    Tincture of clarity 67
    Universal flowering 28
Blood and fire 42
Blooming elixir 23
Bounty's bramble 49
bourbon
    Courage's forge 53
    Inner ward 37
    Invocation 93
    Sage's sipper 59
brandy
    Fortuna 81
    Midwinter mulled
    wine 31
    Sabbath sangaree 38
Butterfly pea gin 122

C

calvados, Draught of
    courage 34

Campari
    Duality 16
    Fruit of foresight 72
    Solar ray 45
Chai syrup 133
Chalice of Eros 20
Chambord, Serenity's
    hatching 115
Chamomile gin 126
cherry brandy, Fruit of
    foresight 72
Cherry gin 124
Cinnamon &
    apple whisky 127
Cinnamon syrup 132
Cleansing fizz 107
coffee liqueur, Spiced
    divination 56
cognac
    Fortuna 81
    Philtre of Venus 24
Courage's forge 53
Coven's ward 108
creme de cacao, Philtre of
    Venus 24
creme de fraise des bois,
    Liquid luck 90
creme de menthe, Coven's
    ward 108
creme de mure, Bounty's
    bramble 49
creme de noyaux, Philtre of
    Venus 24
creme de violette,
    Blooming elixir 23
Cynar, Witches'
    boulevardier 50

D

Dragon's dram 64
Draught of courage 34
Duality 16

F

falernum liqueur, Lucky
    zombie 97

Fire sparker 19
Fortuna 81
Fruit of foresight 72

G

Garden charm 116
Garden of delight 85
gin
    Blooming elixir 23
    Bounty's bramble 49
    Butterfly pea gin 122
    Chamomile gin 126
    Cherry gin 124
    Cleansing fizz 107
    Coven's ward 108
    Garden of delight 85
    Grimoire gimlet 119
    Hex breaker 112
    Mind's eye 60
    Mulberry gin 122
    New beginnings 27
    Prophecy's scent 68
    Rhea's touch 100
    Serenity's hatching 115
    Sloe gin 123
    Solar ray 45
    Solstice sparkler 12
    Sweet harmony 103
    Tranquil waters 104
    Universal flowering 28
Ginger tequila 126
grenadine, Lucky
    zombie 97
Grimoire gimlet 119

H

Harvest 78
hazelnut liqueur
    Invocation 93
    Waking martini 75
Hex breaker 112
High sun 89
Honey syrup 128
Honeysuckle syrup 131

I

Inner ward 37
Invocation 93

L

Lavender syrup 129
Lillet Blanc
Hex breaker 112
New beginnings 27
limoncello, Midsummer
spritz 82
Liquid luck 90
Lucky zombie 97

M

Marigold syrup 132
mezcal
Duality 16
Harvest 78
Tincture of clarity 67
Midsummer spritz 82
Midwinter mulled wine 31
Mind's eye 60
Mulberry gin 122

N

New beginnings 27
Nixta corn liqueur,
Harvest 78
nocino, Inner ward 37

P

peach nectar, Scrying glass
fizz 63
pear liqueur, Garden of
delight 85
Persephone's breath 94
Philtre of Venus 24
Pineapple rum 124
port, Prophecy's scent 68

R

Rhea's touch 100
Rose syrup 129
Rosemary syrup 130

rum

Dragon's dram 64
Liquid luck 90
Lucky zombie 97
Pineapple rum 124
Spiced rum 125
Transfixer 15

S

Sabbath sangaree 38
Saffron syrup 133
Sage's sipper 59
sake, Samhain martini 71
Scrying glass fizz 63
Serenity's hatching 115
sherry, Inner ward 37
Simple syrup 128
Sloe gin 123
Solar ray 45
Solstice sparkler 12
Spiced brew 41
Spiced divination 56
Spiced rum 125
St-Germain
Garden charm 116
Hex breaker 112
Suze, New beginnings 27
Sweet harmony 103

T

tequila
Alignment 46
Blood and fire 42
Fire sparker 19
Ginger tequila 126
High sun 89
Invitation, The 86
Thyme syrup 130
Tincture of clarity 67
Tranquil waters 104
Transfixer 15
triple sec
Blood and fire 42
Blooming elixir 23
Fortuna 81
High sun 89
Persephone's
breath 94

Prophecy's scent 68
Samhain martini 71

U

Universal flowering 28

V

Vanilla syrup 131
vermouth
Fruit of foresight 72
Inner ward 37
Sage's sipper 59
Solar ray 45
Universal flowering 28
Witches'
boulevardier 50
vodka
As above, so below 111
Chalice of Eros 20
Garden charm 116
Invitation, The 86
Midsummer spritz 82
Spiced brew 41
Waking martini 75

W

Waking martini 75
whisky
Cinnamon & apple
whisky 127
Witches' boulevardier 50
wine
Coven's ward 108
Garden of delight 85
Invitation, The 86
Midwinter mulled
wine 31
Sabbath sangaree 38
Scrying glass fizz 63
Solstice sparkler 12
Sweet harmony 103
Witches' boulevardier 50

Z

Zucca, Duality 16

Published in 2025 by Smith Street Books
Naarm (Melbourne) | Australia
smithstreetbooks.com

Distributed outside of ANZ, North & Latin America by Thames & Hudson Ltd.,
6–24 Britannia Street, London, WC1X 9JD
thamesandhudson.com

EU Authorised Representative: Interart S.A.R.L.
19 rue Charles Auray, 93500 Pantin, Paris, France
productsafety@thameshudson.co.uk; www.interart.fr

ISBN: 978-1-9232-3915-9

All rights reserved. No part of this book may be reproduced or transmitted by any person or entity, in any form or by any means, electronic or mechanical, including photocopying, recording, scanning or by any storage and retrieval system, without the prior written permission of the publishers and copyright holders.

Smith Street Books respectfully acknowledges the Wurundjeri People of the Kulin Nation, who are the Traditional Owners of the land on which we work, and we pay our respects to their Elders past and present.

Copyright recipes, text & design © Smith Street Books
Copyright illustrations © Kelly Smith

The moral right of the author has been asserted.

Publisher: Hannah Koelmeyer
Project Editor: Avery Hayes
Editor: Sophie Dougall
Text: Nadia Bailey
Design concept & layout: Francesca Corsini
Illustrations: Kelly Smith
Proofreader: Pam Dunne
Indexer: Max McMaster
Production manager: Aisling Coughlan

Printed & bound in China by C&C Offset Printing Co., Ltd.

Book 404
10 9 8 7 6 5 4 3 2 1